FRILUFTSLIV

CONNECT WITH NATURE
THE NORWEGIAN WAY
FRILUFTSLIV

OLIVIER LUKE DELORIE

STERLING ETHOS
New York

STERLING ETHOS
New York

An Imprint of Sterling Publishing Co., Inc.
1166 Avenue of the Americas
New York, NY 10036

© 2020 Quarto Publishing PLC,
an imprint of The Quarto Group

ISBN 978-1-4549-3920-7

Distributed in Canada by Sterling Publishing Co., Inc.,
c/o Canadian Manda Group,
664 Annette Street, Toronto, Ontario
M6S 2C8, Canada

For information about custom editions, special sales,
and premium and corporate purchases, please contact
Sterling Special Sales at 800-805-5489
or specialsales@sterlingpublishing.com.

Manufactured in Singapore

10 9 8 7 6 5 4 3 2 1

sterlingpublishing.com

For picture credits, see page 160

MIX
Paper from
responsible sources
FSC® C016973

CONTENTS

INTRODUCTION

———

The concept of *friluftsliv* (pronounced free-loofts-LEEV and translated as "open-air living") is not necessarily about climbing and conquering the highest mountains or recklessly racing across sand dunes (though both of these hair-raising activities fit within its definition). You don't need to gear up to go outside, nor hire a guide, nor buy a GPS.

In his 1859 poem "Paa Vidderne," Norwegian playwright Henrik Ibsen expresses the concept of living a "free air life" as our basic human need to be outside and connect with nature. He describes the need for time in solitude in nature to clarify one's thoughts. Evolutionary biologist Professor Hans Gelter says "genuine friluftsliv is finding your way home to nature; being in nature not for an activity, but just to be there."

Closely connected with the idea of friluftsliv is the freedom to roam. All Scandinavian countries—as evidenced by the 1957 Outdoor Recreation Act—allow free access to walk or camp anywhere you like, as long as you respect both locals and wildlife. Termed *allemannsretten* ("everyman's right") in Norway, this open-air philosophy cannot help but encourage exploration, adventure, and a lifelong respect for the environment.

In celebrating the sentiment of friluftsliv, this book aims to (re)align your values and priorities; for the natural rhythms of your body, mind, and spirit find harmony—a feeling of home—when they are in nature. We endeavor to remind you of what is important and guide you toward the inner peace you seek by (re)turning your attention to such simple acts as simply sitting in the grass and listening.

According to UN listings, Scandinavian countries consistently rank as the happiest countries on Earth, so perhaps it's time to rekindle the spirit of friluftsliv in your life—no matter where you live—and break down the physical (and figurative) walls standing between you and the natural wonders of the world.

May you experience both the awesome and astonishing while deciphering the humble and simple, and may your (un)conscious desire to nurture a sacred relationship with nature be roused and awakened.

Oliver Luke Delorie

1

JUST BE

You don't need anything to friluftsliv but open the door, step outside, and take a deep breath. This chapter will remind you in fifteen elementary ways that friluftsliv can also be a verb, as in "I'm going friluftsliving."

Sit Still

———

Unless it is instinctual to you, choosing to leave comfortable modern conveniences and set out into the big world beyond our walls and roofs is often driven by nagging feelings of necessity. Uncontrollably drawn into action, we are compelled by unconscious desires to distract ourselves from simply sitting still and doing nothing. The next time you are happily relaxing on your favorite log, park bench, or the peak of a majestic mountain you spent days climbing, resist the temptation to move on to the next thing until you have been there without a care for anything but fresh air. You will find stillness that rivals that of a Scandinavian spa.

Smell the Roses

While attending to our responsibilities and the duties
of our day-to-day lives, we can easily forget to focus on
the delicate details designed to delight us. They appear
everywhere, in every shape, form, and guise. The trick is to
refine your powers of observation—via repeated effort—and
acknowledge the magic Mother Nature has conjured for you
to connect with on some level (be it emotional, physical, or
spiritual). Every second spent out-of-doors will fuse your
mind, body, and spirit with an appreciation of nature's
magnificence made manifest. It is quietly whispering for
you to pay attention. Are you listening?

WATER

———

Drink it from a cool, clear creek or from your
water bottle; watch it evaporate, turn into vapor,
and shape itself into clouds; marvel at its fluid, molten
nature as it crashes against craggy rocks or laps lazily
at your toes at the calm edge of a shore. Visualize the
immensity of near-endless oceans stretched across time
so vast the next stops are distant lands; melt under the
pounding pulse of a waterfall. Liquid and frozen, H_2O is
a crucial component in the construction of every living
thing on Earth, a meat-and-potatoes miracle to be
celebrated, cherished, and conserved.

Grass Nap

———

In season, lawns are like lush, soft-shag carpets. Their terrestrial thermostats are set just right to cool you off and provide much-needed relief from the heat. When was the last time you laid down long enough to fall asleep in a green meadow without a worry? Whether you like to conk out and snore on your back, toss and turn on your tummy, or curl up snug and cozy on your side, keep a wool or fleece blanket tucked in the trunk of your car because you never know when spontaneous grass naps can happen.

Get Perspective

If you enjoy taking photographs, you have experienced perspective via the viewfinder that either connects—or disconnects—you from the objects you are observing. How does the distance between you and your subject change your approach to capturing images? Cameras are common companions on outdoor outings; when you bring yours along, do you find that the technology drags you deeper into a distorted (artistic) view of reality? Or does the zoom function allow you to focus your aim and commune with what you shoot in a more intimate way?

Feel the Breeze

Depending where you live, midsummer winds
either appear as friend or foe; they may be lovely and
fragrant, flowering with the sweet scent of fruit-tree
blossoms, or they may hint at the cool, crisp colors of the
fall harvest that find orchards bursting with juicy grapes,
crunchy apples, and crispy pears. Norway itself rests on the
edge of the Arctic Circle in a polar vortex of low pressure
that produces wind so swift and brisk it can whisk you away.
What will you make of the breeze blowing by your sun-
creamed—or turtle-necked—neck of the woods the
next time a zephyr of wind whispers in your
ear when you least expect it?

WATCH THE SUN RISE AND SET

—

From the first light of a new day to the final
farewell of nightfall, we worship in wonder the big
flashlight in the sky in all its glowing glory. It grows our
grapes so that we may make wine; it guides and enhances
our experience as we gallivant across the globe; and it gives
us the warmth we need to flourish and grow. These sunrises
and sunsets mirror the two most miraculous moments of
our lives. Try this experiment the next time you want a
reminder of the (in)significance of existence: pretend
your life lasted a single day; be there at the moment
you are born, and then again when you pass away.

The Breath of Life

—

Unless you are working up a sweat, your brain may forget
you are a living, breathing human being. The simple act
of paying attention to the rhythm of your breath will put
you into a mindful, meditative state of present-moment
awareness that is only otherwise experienced while
exercising. If you're lucky enough to be filling your lungs
with fresh Norwegian air, you can breathe even easier
knowing this country is a zero-emission leader.
As you wander the wilds of your closest countryside,
private paddocks, or farmlands further afield, seeking
to soak up the ecstatically euphoric ecstasy of your
environment, remember that with every inhalation you
are connecting with everything around you, and
with every exhalation you are letting it go.

> **"** If you truly love nature, you will find beauty everywhere. **"**

Vincent van Gogh, artist

PACK LIGHT

—

Few friluftsliv adventures can rival a trek to Romsdalseggen ridge, one of the most beautiful hikes in Norway. Be sure to plan well though—no one enjoys lugging a heavy pack around all day. Wherever you're heading, when you arrive at the perfect paradise, you don't want to ruin the marvelous moment cursing your sack of stuff instead of gazing in reverence at the gorgeous view before you. If you'd rather not spend the rest of your life visiting your chiropractor on a regular basis, carefully consider what you bring with you on your next voyage. Every ounce counts; you want to be leaping fences in single bounds, not falling face-first in the dirt.

Let Your Mind Wander

If you dream of going somewhere you haven't
been before—yet prefer planning your great adventures
from the comfort of your rocking chair—your mind is
your best friend. All adventures—both physical and
metaphysical—begin between your ears. We envision
crumbling castles high on hillsides; the wind in our sails
as we cross tranquil seas; and the sound of music wafting
over us as we wander through idyllic mountain meadows.
Let the wistful wanderings that tug on your heartstrings
lead and guide you out into the world of wonder so you
can experience how free your life can be.

Peek Over the Edge

The experienced adventurer performs an elegant swan dive
from the clifftop into the warm, clear blue water below and
barely makes a splash. It appears a feat fit only for an
Olympian from Mount Olympus itself. For the more
cautious, crawling like a snail on our bellies up to the edge
of the ridge and taking a look at what lies beneath—all from
the safety of our risk-free roost—seems like the saner
option. Keep your center of gravity low as you approach
(especially if it's windy) and leave the thrill-seeking to
the adrenaline junkies . . . unless you are one!

Gaze at the Moon

The moon has been orbiting the sun—just like us—since before time began ticking. It enchants us with its waxing and waning, tugging on our tides and inspiring sensitive song lyrics. When hidden by our 870,000 mile (1,400,000 km) shadow, we see galaxies twinkle with memories of stardust traveling at the speed of light. When the moon sees the sun again, we see its slender sliver denoting the beginning of a new phase. And as its view increases, we see even more of its cosmic face until its lunar light shines at its zenith, inspiring tide-turning madness in all who are made of water.

LISTEN TO BIRDS

—

Tweeting used to conjure contemplative
thoughts of birds wooing their mates with sweet songs.
World over, they still whistle and coo high in the treetops
transmitting their memos and missives to kith and kin.
(If only they knew how we've co-opted this notion—
hopefully we haven't ruffled their feathers too much.)
Listen and delight in the cadence of their catchy melodies;
their arpeggiated warbles accent the wee hours of early
morning before the sun has even woken up.

Walk

When you walk, you allow your thoughts to think for themselves (so you can enjoy some peace and quiet for once). Your body loves to move in gentle ways that stretch your muscles, even just slightly. When your blood starts flowing, you begin to perceive the perpetual patchwork of psychic input around you, so the more you meander through—and align yourself with—nature, the more you become a magnet for new ideas. What shape do these take? That's up to you. Only you know what you are searching for when you walk out your door.

2

PLAY

If you can't remember the last time you did something and didn't care what anyone thought about it, this chapter will help you rekindle the joys of amusing yourself and the people you love in and with nature.

Let Your Inner Animal Out

If you could shape-shift into any animal,
what critter or creature would you morph into?
Have you ever imagined silently stalking your supper
on your hands and knees about to pounce? Or lazing the
day away nuzzled in the nook of your favorite tree like a
sleepy sloth? What would life be like as a polar bear on the
far-flung Svalbard archipelago 500 miles (800 km) north of
the Norwegian mainland? The next time you're out and
about in the boonies and feeling playful, imagine you are
your favorite beast or bug and bounce around like Tigger
or slither soundlessly through the tall grass like a king
cobra looking for a mongoose to mess with.

ROCK HOUND

—

The most sluggish of aggregate mineral matter,
rocks make up the outer layer of Earth's crust and have
fascinated petrologists (rock scientists) since the first
of the crust-curious among us began their studies. If you
are inclined toward geology and the thought of hunting,
gathering, tumbling, cutting, grinding, polishing, and
finishing these hard and heavy gems and minerals into
jewelry and other forms of petrified, fossilized art turns
your body to stone—as if Medusa herself gave you
"the look"—then join a club and head out on a weekend
field trip. Leave your amateur lapidary (rock artist)
mark behind via pebble graffiti. For example, write
on a light-colored rock using a dark one.

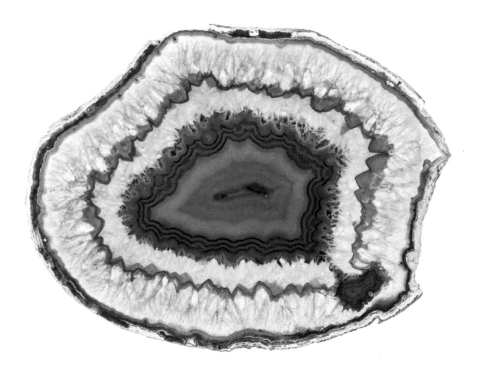

Gather Seashells

Don't worry your pretty little head about Suzie;
she went out of business long ago after confusing
countless would-be customers with her tongue-twisting
alliterations. There are plenty of perfectly sandblasted
seashells waiting for you half-buried in the sand. When
the water is too cold to swim and the wind too swift to
play catch, lay claim to your own pieces of paradise that
were once tiny homes to slug-slow undersea creatures
and fashion your finds into a piece of jewelry, a soap
dish, a candle holder, or ornaments for a tree.

Tidal Pools

Tidal pools teem with a medley of marine life in such abundance that it is difficult to find anything quite like these micro-ecosystems anywhere else on Earth. Bat stars, sea stars, sea urchins, and crusty crustaceans live among microscopic aquatic life-forms that all battle to survive pounding waves and temperatures that fluctuate faster than your partner's mood on a cloudy, coffee-less, misty morning. In Norway, the fairy-tale ponds in the region of Sanna flourish under around-the-clock sun every summer, so time the tides and explore where the ocean meets the land. What better way to spend the day than respectfully splashing around a fishy fishbowl depicting life under the sea that only you—curious and adventurous—get to see?

HAVE A
WATER FIGHT

———

Fun is fleeting, so frolic with folly, absorbing it like
a sponge when it spills out and flows over you and the
people you love. When you all tire of jumping through
the sprinkler (and if squirting and splashing those you
care about most with liquid sunshine is a highlight of
summer), switch to water guns and position yourself near
the supply so you can reload without blinking; the last
thing you want is to be cornered by the kids and be
shooting blanks. If this happens—and you are still
standing by the faucet—grab the hose, squeeze
the trigger, and drench everyone in sight.

" It is a happy
talent to know
how to play. **"**

—

Ralph Waldo Emerson, poet

Slide Down a Hill

———

Hills are sloped and slippery for a reason. Whether powdered with snow or covered in green grass or acres of sand, they were made for sleds in all shapes and sizes. Use a piece of waxed cardboard if you must, but to the bottom you must go. Do some calculations and "know before you go," strapping on your skis, snowboard, or sandboard and barrel down (or gingerly sidestep) your way to the bottom of the slope before you. What lies ahead? A green-means-go bunny hill? A you-better-know-what-you're-doing double black diamond run? Hopefully something more suitable to your skill and ability lies between the two. Of course, if you prefer the padding of your bottom, you can always go *aking* (Norwegian for tobogganing) instead.

Your Big Year

———

There's such a thing as a Big Year—an informal competition among birders who attempt to identify as many species as possible by sight or sound, within a single calendar year and within a specific geographic area. Made popular in North America, initially by scouring a single state or province (or all of them), the world record for 365 days stands at 6,852. If you're charmed by our feathered friends, lift your wings and fly! Fledgling ornithologists would do well to head to northern Norway to add puffins, kittiwakes, auks, guillemots, and cormorants to their lists.

Make a
Daisy Chain

———

Any florist will tell you there are flowers for every occasion. And royalty will tell you any occasion is an opportunity for glitzy jewelry (no ceremony is complete without handmade crown, wrist and ankle bracelets, and rings for kings or queens themselves). Pick a bouquet of daisies, and with a steady hand—and the precision of a surgeon—carefully make an incision in the center of the stem, near the end, with the tip of your finest fingernail. Now string your posy of daisies together and flaunt your floral riches in style as you prance across a red carpet of grass, dancing in the dappled sunlight.

Make Music

The pulsating hum of a gas-powered leaf blower can sound like music to some. So can the high-pitched wind whistling through slender clarinet-like reeds in a marshy bog. Think of woodpeckers as jazz drummers and whales as the baritone tuba section in the symphony orchestra of nature. Create a spontaneous concert performance by pounding (or tapping) out a rhythm with two weighted sticks and imitate the scratch of the washboard-like *güiro* as you run a twig over a pine cone. Finally, call a camp meeting to order by blowing into a conch shell, beckoning all with its bellow. Will they listen? Depends on how much you have been practicing.

Sketch

If the house is spotless and the kids have been excitedly whisked away for the weekend—and you have always imagined yourself as an artist—toss a handful of their crayons, chalk, or colored pencils and blank paper in a bag (or stop at the art supply–laden discount store) and head for the beach, rain forest, or pine bluff to find a quiet spot. In your mind's eye, begin by tracing the shape of any structure, surface, or contour that catches your attention. Now try the same thing on paper. You don't need anyone's stamp of approval but your own.

Skip Stones

———

Stones don't float, as you may have noticed.
But we don't give up trying to keep them leaping and
hopping on the surface of water, regardless of the outcome.
The name of the game is to beat your own personal record
by throwing a flat-as-you-can-find stone across a body of
water with a quick side-arm flick and counting the number
of times it bounces before it sinks. By comparison, lobbing
lowly pebbles into a pond can lead to pondering the
meaning of life as the wavy ripples
dissolve into nothing.

WILDCRAFTING

Throughout the untamed wilderness of your
neighborhood exist countless uncultivated plants and
herbs you can harvest and juice into liquids, mix into
medicine, and steep into tonics, teas, and tinctures.
You may walk by edible and medicinal plants every day,
so keep your eyes peeled like grapes because what may
appear as weeds may also be wellsprings of well-being.
Find a local guide who can teach you the difference between
the edible and the toxic lookalikes (of which there are
plenty) and get a book to help identify each. Finally,
ask permission to pick before crafting your perfumed batch
of potpourri from plants growing on private plots of land.

Build a Sandcastle

Once you have carefully constructed the minarets of your sandcastle, make sure you dig a moat and bury any potential invaders lurking nearby up to their necks in the same stuff. The last thing you want is to sustain any damage or have said marauders demolish the new residence of future random sand dwellers, who will find comfort and solace in your tunnels and turrets. Norway humbly boasts the second-longest coastline in the world, providing free reign to stack, stomp, and smooth your citadel of sand anywhere you like. If you want the sands of time to be kind to your castle and ensure it stands the test of tides, adhere to your local oceanic zoning department's setback requirements (i.e. don't build it too close to the water's edge).

3

CONTEMPLATE

To contemplate is to be inquisitive
about something without thinking too
hard about it. This chapter will support
your efforts to simply observe and
appreciate all nature has to offer.

Make a Pilgrimage

Traditionally, believers parade their way to places of personal spiritual significance such as Mecca, Assisi, or the Camino de Santiago to sanctify the beliefs of their chosen faith and honor their commitment to the principles of their ideology. Seekers of all sorts searching for a sense of enlightenment walk for days (instead of taking the train or braving long-distance buses). If you're on a personal pilgrimage in Norway, allow patron saint Olaf to guide you and listen for a happy *hei-hei* (pronounced "hi") that will brighten your day on your way to your next night in modest accommodations. What humble heritage site summons you with a sacred crusade on two feet?

Strengthen Your Connection

If you have ever shed sorrowful tears over
the nagging feeling you don't belong on Earth,
that you are existentially lost, that the mothership left
before beaming you back up, accept this tragic fact and
adapt to your new environment. (If no one has noticed
you're missing by now, take advantage of the fact it may
be a while before they come back.) Every breath and every
step offers an opportunity to (re)connect with where and
who and what you are. Find comfort (*hygga*), the root
of mood (*hugr*), in the fundamental foundations and
essential elements that inspire you to establish contact.
Explore them and Earth will finally feel like home.

GO GEOCACHING

If your imagination regularly ran away as a child whenever you pored over fictional fables of fearless fortune hunters seeking sunken riches, or real-life accounts of brave and bold adventurers digging for buried treasure beside an old tree, you can now get in on the action. Using GPS and your natural navigational skills, geocachers play hide-and-seek in search of loot (also known as caches) located in various locales the world over. But be careful: friluftsliv-inspired geo fever is incurable; you may never want to stay inside again.

The Bark of a Tree

———

Similar to our own skin, the outermost layers
of trees, vines, and shrubs not only protect these woody
plants from scorching sun and mighty winds, they also
provide shelter for insects, moss, and fungi. Furthermore,
many mammals (including humans) eat not the sweet and
brittle bark found in candy shops, but the inner skin of most
pines, slippery elms, black and yellow birch, and red and
black spruce (all considered edible plants). So close your
eyes and carefully caress the textural nooks and crannies
of tough tree bark on your coming travels; it may awaken
(or restore) your extrasensory awareness of the
essential biodiversity of the forest.

Pick Up Trash

—

Regardless of how you feel about the
garbage-pail-dwelling, green-carpeted grouch
from Sesame Street, all wise woodland wanderers,
bright beach-bumming backpackers, and carbon emission-
offsetting globe-trotting gallivanters exploring the Earth
know that we must protect our planet. "Take only photos or
memories, leave only footprints" and "pack it in, pack it out"
are mottos to follow, for you know—as a seeker of freedom,
independence, and experience in the great outdoors—it is
everyone's responsibility to preserve the character and
complexion of the countryside (and cosmos) for future
generations not wanting to migrate to Mars.

Leave a Trail of Breadcrumbs

How else will you know where to go when you get
lost because you didn't download or update the offline
map and your phone powers itself off to conserve what
juice it has left? Many birds eat half of their body weight
a day, so if you're thinking they will surely pass on your
scattered dark rye breadcrumbs, specs of day-old sourdough
spelt, or pungent caraway seeds, you are mistaken. There
are other ways to remember where you've been: bring a
compass and a physical map, learn celestial navigation
(connect the dots of constellations), and tell someone
if you are skedaddling off the beaten track.

P.S. Bring a loaf of fjellbrød just for fun.

Shimmering Spider Silk

———

When it's dry, the necklace-like structure of spider
silk—five times stronger than steel in density—functions
at its best, capturing food for our often-feared eight-legged
friends. Even though humans marvel at a web's ability to
collect moisture from the air, spiders aren't too happy about
it. When a web is drenched in water droplets, it's difficult to
bring home the bacon. But as the sun slowly warms the
Earth as it rises higher in the sky, our glimpse of glistening
morning dew also evaporates, ensuring the elegant
gossamer latticework returns to work and meets
its daily quota. See if you can find one.

ADOPT A PET ROCK

Go outside and pick a rock, any rock. Now pick up a paintbrush, dip it in paint, and play. Unless you are the type to place it carefully in your coat or pants pocket and carry it with you everywhere you go, the low-maintenance domesticated stone will likely be perfectly happy sitting on your windowsill or bedside table (just as long as it can see you and you can see it). If your pebble pet ever gets lonely, make it a companion. Heck, why not create an entire village and name them all? In public and in private, everyone has their quirks, so foster as many pet rocks as you can responsibly parent.

Your Nature Spirit

The mischievous, elemental spiritual beings pulling
the strings behind all things in nature come in all shapes
and sizes, and all are tasked with a unique job description.
Each ensures the endurance of Earth's ecology. Only once
your third eye has been activated will you be able to even
comprehend (let alone be told) the secret password to open
fairy doors to other dimensions. But if you can't wait for an
enlightened elf to offer his or her imaginary hand and whisk
you off to never-never land, imagine yourself shrinking into
a sprightly sprite and doing what your *hulder* (wood nymph)
would do given free reign to run amok in
the wildest of woods.

❝ I like this place and could willingly waste my time in it. ❞

—

William Shakespeare, playwright,

As You Like It

Magical Mushrooms

Not to be confused with the psychedelic
variety (whose chemical composition summons
demons whilst simultaneously revealing one's life's
purpose via the dissolution of every real and imagined
barrier between all living things), the sane among us
trust in the secular pastime of fungi identification.
The last thing you want is to go on a one-way trip.
Knowing upon which toadstools to sit is crucial
(so get a manual to identify them) because edible
mushrooms such as "chicken of the woods" are
divinely delicious when fried in garlic and butter.

Make a Crop Circle

Cereologists (people who study crop circles)
believe the masterminds behind these mathematical,
geometric designs made of bent wheat and barley are simply
stalk-stomping ufologists who employ rope, ladders, and
planks of wood to deceive and delight us. It appears as if
a gazillion strands of grass have been flash-steamed—at
precise angles—between sunset and sunrise. If you get good
at producing these spellbinding spectacles that seem sent
from the stars, don't let us in on your celestial secrets.
Keep us bewildered and enchanted.

WINTER
SCAVENGER HUNT

—

A game of grit and resolve, a scavenger hunt conjures
memories of rummaging for, and rooting out, items on the
list your mom gave you on a warm sunny day during
summer vacation. But now you're an adult and what is there
to find in wintertime? First, fill a thermos with hot coffee,
cocoa, or *gløgg* (Norwegian mulled wine spiced with
cinnamon, cloves, and cardamom). Now gather together
family and friends and bribe them to brainstorm an
itemized list of seasonally inspired loot to scavenge.
If this is a solo venture, ask yourself the existential
question: What am I looking for, and
why am I looking for it?

Turn Over
a New Leaf

———

Designed primarily with the aim of permitting
photosynthesis, humans eat a variety of leaves and
also wrap, steam, cook, spice, and flavor food with them.
We dry and steep this foliage into afternoon tea, and create
aromatherapeutic oils by extracting their essences.
When you find yourself ambling through any green space,
treat yourself to an impromptu aromatherapy session.
Pick a leaf of a plant you are drawn to, tear it open,
and hold it up to your nose. Close your eyes and breathe
in the fragrant perfume. What does it smell like?
What does it remind you of? Experiment with new
leaves until you find one that smells just right.

4

EXPLORE EXPERIENCE

There are as many ways to explore the world as there are people and personalities, and with exploring comes experience. The ideas in this chapter will encourage you to get outside and get a breath of "free air."

The Ends
of the Earth

While you can get to the South Pole by land, the North Pole is in the middle of the Arctic Ocean. The distance between the two—from one end of Earth to the other—is only 8,595.35 miles (13,832.88 km) so unless you live on the equator, you are closer to one of them. Standing in serene silence on the top (or bottom) of the world on an Arctic or Antarctic expedition is a feeling you won't get from a book or film (it will be compiled by people for whom this excursion has become routine). Are you up for an extraordinary endeavor future polar navigator?

STRIKE IT RICH

All living things—animate and inanimate—exist for your pleasure and amusement, to be relished and cherished, coveted and preserved. You decide what matters to you, and in what quality and quantity. Your values determine how prosperous you feel, and your resources depend only upon your belief in their existence. Whether metaphorically or literally, we are all on a quest for gold in the rushing riverbed of life. Whether you hike to the Klondike with pan in hand to stake your claim or luxuriate in the abundant natural beauty surrounding you, you will always strike a vein of gold when you recognize the riches around you.

Sleep in a Hammock

After stomping your way over stumps and logs or plodding through thickets, trying your best not to slip or trip when all you want to do is take a snoozy siesta, let the wind rock your comfy cradle gently back and forth, turn the timberland or taiga into a breezy bedroom, and hang your hammock between two trees. Ideally, its shape and size suit your shape and size (you tested it at home before stuffing it into your kit and sticking out your thumb to hitch a lift, right?). Your circadian rhythms change based on increasing daylight the farther north you go, so bring an eye mask to be sure that you get some restful shut-eye.

ANOTHER WORLD

—

Close your eyes for a minute and imagine you
have just landed on a new planet. You have been tasked
with exploring and documenting your findings for the
rest of us. You have never been here before, and everything
you see and feel and hear is new to you. What is the first
thing you do? Observe, explore, touch, listen, and play.
Encounter the people, food, language, architecture,
philosophy, climate, and geography with an open mind
and a patient heart. Now open your eyes and go
somewhere you have never been before.

Shelter from the Storm

Crawl into a cave, nestle into the nook of a big old
oak tree, or fashion your own shelter using branches,
boughs, and bits of whatever you can find. Try twisting
the tender willow tendrils into a mat or recliner and
upholster them with squishy moss to make your temporary
home feel cozier. You can always create a comfortable
place if you are creative and clever—you don't need
resources to be resourceful. Settle in and count the
imaginary sheep playfully leaping over your
grass-covered hut as you find safety and security
in the sanctuary-like stillness of your short-term digs.

Fly Like a Bird

———

Humans have dreamt of sprouting wings and flying since we saw birds doing it. Flying a kite, kite surfing, hang-gliding, paragliding, or packing and pulling a parachute from your backpack as you fall to Earth all satisfy an eon-long desire to hover among the clouds, lifted and lofted by wind and creative contraption (like the actor who tied a bunch of helium-filled balloons to a chair and lifted off, not knowing he was headed for a happy ending). If dreams of fabulous flying inspire you to jump into the jet stream and soar like an eagle, get the proper training, go with a guide, and take wing!

" The clearest way into the Universe is through a forest wilderness. "

John Muir, naturalist and author

Two Wheels

Everywhere you can go on four wheels you can
go on two (some of the best camping and hiking spots
can only be accessed on two circles; four just don't fit).
Where do you want to go? And how do you want to get
there? "Four wheels move the body and two wheels move
the soul," say advocates of dividing your wheelbase by two.
Unless you already commute or tour by bicycle—and have
thus been converted to the church of tandem travel—
remember that bikes run on fat and save you money,
while cars run on money and can make you fat.

GROW YOUR OWN FOOD

Growing your own food is one of life's greatest pleasures. Not only will you feel more secure knowing where your food comes from, and that you will always have enough, you will become more invested in the health of your family, friends, and neighbors. Your fruits, vegetables, and other products fuel the loving labors and empowering endeavors of everyone you share time with. Whether you communally plan and plant a community garden or simply grow a few of your favorite herbs on your balcony, you cannot feed the people you care about most with what you grew in your garden without pondering the paramount importance and purpose of plants in your life.

Float in a Boat

———

Roughly 71 percent of Earth's surface is covered in water, so if you are wind- or powerboat-driven to go where fewer people have gone before, bobbing around on a boat is the way to get there. You can cross oceans on a fjord-and-glacier globe-circumnavigating adventure, race your radio-controlled hovercraft on the pond in the park on a Sunday afternoon, or float a tiny toy on a leaf raft from one end of a puddle to the other. However you get out on the water is up to you. Remember: Your sea-faring Arctic ice-breaker is safe behind the breakwater in the harbor, but that's not what you were built for.

Track Down Dinner

Unless your geography or culture
encourages—or requires—you to hunt and fish to
survive, whacking an animal (and eating it) can be a
moral decision. Either you hunt and fish (and can't imagine
not doing it) or you don't (and can't imagine doing it).
Regardless of which side of the river you pitch your tent,
the celebrated act of gathering is accepted by everyone
camped by the waterway; this activity entails no license,
training, or special gear. Finding and foraging for food with
your own two hands brings rewards commensurate with
your effort, skill, and ability, so ask yourself: What edible
flora and fauna make your mouth water?

Visit a Farm

———

Milk a cow and make yogurt. Hypnotize the chickens and collect their eggs. Muck out the barn and keep the horses happy. Pet the llamas, feed the ducks, and pick out your own pumpkin. Prune raspberry canes and hack down blackberry bushes. Stomp this year's grapes as you sip the nectar of last year's harvest. A farm tour is an outdoor party and everyone in nature is invited. You will get dirty while making new friends. And when you're strategically balanced on a ladder picking plump purple plums high in a tree, feel free to sing "one for the bucket and one for me."

Honor the Ocean

———

The ocean roars and purrs as it rises and falls.
The waves wash over you and salt pickles you as grains
of sand stick to your skin. Hug your surfboard or boogie
board and wait for the perfect surge of water to propel you
forward, rather than trying to keep your balance by burying
your feet in the turbulent quicksand whose shifting current
can instantly imbalance you. Revere the (metaphorical) sea,
ride its ripples, and it will eventually settle and float you
safely to shore. Simply breathe as if you are in sync with
the rhythmic cadence of life's cascading waves, even if you
are just making your way along The Atlantic Road in
Norway, dubbed the most beautiful drive in the world.

Light Your Fire

———

What sparks your inner flame? What fuels the blaze
once it catches fire and starts burning? Your daydreams
and burning desires you conjure and admire in your head
and in your heart can only take shape in the external, outer
world of form and function. Go outside, for you will meet
them on the trail, see them in the stars, and feel them in the
breeze. On your next outdoor overnight, let the flickering
flames that light up the night leap and illuminate the
shadows where your fears lie. Now that you can see them,
they can't hide. Follow your firelight and run wild.

5

SIMPLE
PLEASURES

You know deep down inside the cockles
of your heart and in the corners of your
soul that fun, friends, freedom, and love
are better when brought together in nature.
This chapter will jog your memory.

Make Every Day Earth Day

―――

Pledging to celebrate our planet—and our connection to it—creates a conscious bond not only between us and Earth, but also between each other. Rekindling our relationship with the source of life that sustains, feeds, waters, warms, shelters, excites, and challenges us ought to be a daily ritual. From sea to sky, without land and the protective cocoon of our atmosphere we would not survive a second. And without gratitude and reverence for all living things we will either lose our home, or it will lose us. Promise to honor the planet and it will faithfully honor you.

Under the Midnight Sun

At the equator, day and night are equal all year,
but as you approach the North Pole, summer days linger
longer, allowing you the opportunity to frolic or reflect as
day turns to dusk, and then to dark, whose time this season
is short. As the sun dips beneath the horizon, you find
comfort knowing it won't be long before a new day dawns
again. The farther north you go, the longer the light show.
Watch the parties and pleasure endure with merry measure
into the wee hours as you and your loved ones celebrate
the twilight between darkness and daylight.

Play in the Rain

———

Warm rain is welcome relief on a hot and dry
sun-drenched day; it's like the first spray of a sprinkler
when the hose has been sitting in the sun soaking up solar
rays all day. If you fend off winter every year, your big
umbrella, high-priced rain gear, and duck mind-set are your
best friends. But what about the rest of us featherless,
non-down-filled humans who fear tears falling from heaven?
Instead of curling up inside listening to the pitter patter on
your roof, go outside and feel the pitter patter on you.
One reason pluviophiles (people who love the rain) are
happier is because sadness doesn't frighten them.

Fall in Abundance

——

In fall, Norway is a paradise "powered by nature."
The crimped and curled brittle brown, red, orange, and
yellow leaves falling to the ground are simply another
timestamp in the seasonal cycle of life. Before slipping into
a melancholic mood, brooding about the passage of time
and the thought that winter is just around the corner, get
out your rake and mark the moment. Cast your mind back
to the time when you were a child and you conjured your
own magic, waiting in patient anticipation while your
mom or dad did all the work stacking the leaves in your
favor. Now your happiness is up to you, so jump in!

GIVE A TREE A HUG

—

Oxytocin bonds you with your favorite things,
and dopamine makes you feel good. Put these two heavenly
hormones together and you feel as if you can do anything.
Science shows people are happier, healthier, and more
creative and connected when they spend time with trees.
If ever you haven't met your daily quota for hugs (four for
survival, eight for maintenance, and twelve for growth)
and are feeling unwanted or unloved, head for your
nearest forest. Once you wrap your arms around a giant,
old-growth cedar, you never have to let go. The best part?
Trees of all shapes and sizes will always hug you back.

Get the
Gang Together

———

In 2017, a United Nations committee named Norway "the world's happiest country," with close connection to friends and family being largely responsible. Thanks to technology, you have no excuse not to summon your flock of nearest and dearest to a family or school reunion, your rabble of radical activist associates to a militant meeting of the minds, or your tight-knit congregation of like-minded church-going parishioners to a Sunday-stroll-slash-strawberry-tea. Beckon them from near and far, for all seek to bond via friendship and heritage, find comfort in companionship and comradeship, and worship what they believe in faithful fellowship. Where will you meet and where will you go?

SOAK IN HOT SPRINGS

———

What is more calming and tranquil than melting
in a bubbling bath? Hot water thaws you out and
soothes your sore muscles after a long day on the slopes
(or after days and nights slugging through snowy woods
on snowshoes in search of sanctuary). Whether you
bushwhack your way through a blizzard, blaze a mountain
trail across an Alpine meadow, or follow the beaten path to
the parking lot, relax and let the hot water do what it does
best. Loosen up and put your feet up, because stress and
anxiety weren't given directions to the party.

Walk Barefoot

—

When you imagine going barefoot, do you get flashbacks of walking flat-footed—fueled by hype and light trance—across burning coals at a personal development seminar? Instead, take off your shoes and squeeze cool grass between your toes or sink them into warm, soft sand. How long can you keep your balance when you promenade across a pebbly playground, or hop over a snow bank and plunge into a glacier-fed lake for a bracing dip before tip-toeing back to the hot tub to tingle? Find a foot-safe place to break the ice between you and the floor beneath your feet and revel in the sensations to be had from warm sand, cool earth, or frost-tipped grass.

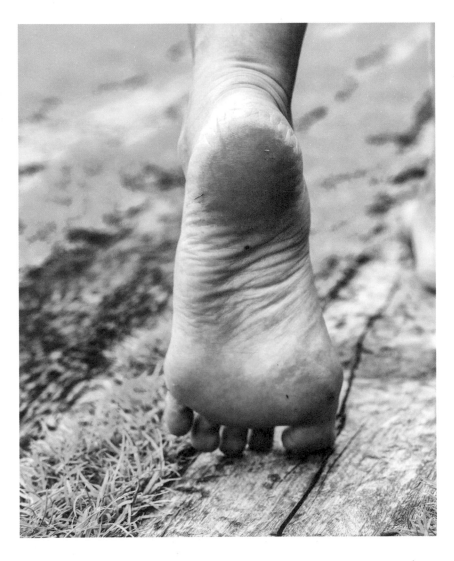

The End of
the Rainbow

———

What lies at the end of the rainbow? Wouldn't you
like to know? So go and find out and tell us all about
it (unless you find a pot of pay dirt piled high with
leprechaunian liquid assets that may be worth something to
someone someday). Unicorns, fairies, and gosh-knows-what-
else surely lurk invisible within the technicolor mist as rain
and sun squabble for supremacy. As you make your way
through the refracted and dispersed light of enchanted
lands, let mythical magic and fabled fairy tales guide you
to your treasure, for what you seek is seeking you.

" Heaven is under our feet as well as over our heads. "

Henry David Thoreau,
essayist, poet, and philosopher

Skinny-dip

———

When you've tried everything and still don't feel
a connection to tangible terra firma or a sense of place
in the unending universe, there is always a body of water,
a way to get there, and the midsummer opportunity to let it
all go. Feel free to feel the folly of baring your beauty in
nothing but your birthday suit. In the nude, in the buff,
take it off. Whatever you call it, it's the most daring,
entertaining, and amusing diversion for fish of all ages
(even stoics stand starkly in awe of luxuriating lunatics as
they dissolve into oneness with water, whatever the
temperature). What are you waiting for? Strip!

Resources

Henderson, Bob, and Nils Vikander. *Nature First: Outdoor Life the Friluftsliv Way*. Toronto: Natural Heritage, 2007.

Hofmann, Annette R., Carsten Gade Rolland, Kolbjørn Rafoss, and Herbert Zoglowek. *Norwegian Friluftsliv: A Way of Living and Learning in Nature*. New York: Waxmann Verlag GmbH, 2018.

Isberg, Roger and Sarah. *Simple Life "Friluftsliv": People Meet Nature*. Bloomington: Trafford Publishing, 2007.

McGurk, Linda Åkeson. *There's No Such Thing as Bad Weather: A Scandinavian Mom's Secrets for Raising Healthy, Resilient, and Confident Kids (from Friluftsliv to Hygge)*. New York: Touchstone Books, 2018.

Muir, John. *John of the Mountains*. Wisconsin: University of Wisconsin Press, 2009.

Thoreau, Henry David. *Walden*. London: Penguin Classics, 2016.

Williams, Florence. *The Nature Fix: Why Nature Makes Us Happier, Healthier, and More Creative*. New York: W. W. Norton & Company, 2017.

Picture Credits

2, 10, 42, 72, 102, 132 Shutterstock/krrow148; 5, 106 Shutterstock/Lukasz Kochanek; 7 Shutterstock/baranq; 8 Shutterstock/justsolove; 13 Shutterstock/Titova Iuliia; 15 Shutterstock/kuni---ka; 16 Shutterstock/PrasongTakham; 17 Shutterstock/Becky Starsmore; 19 Shutterstock/AnjelikaGr; 21 Shutterstock/REDPIXEL.PL; 22 Shutterstock/optimarc; 24 Shutterstock/Yuriy Kulik; 25 Shutterstock/Yury Smelov; 26–27 Shutterstock/fizkes; 29 Shutterstock/Andrew Mayovskyy; 30 Shutterstock/Konstantin Egorychev; 31 Shutterstock/Brian Goodman; 33 Shutterstock/M Vilaret; 35 Shutterstock/evenfh; 36 Shutterstock/kdshutterman; 38 Shutterstock/Vishnevskiy Vasily; 39 Shutterstock/ra3rn; 41 Shutterstock/Lukina Anna; 47 Shutterstock/Dario Lo Presti; 49 Shutterstock/LadyAtlantis; 51 Shutterstock/Robert D Young; 52 Shutterstock/mykhailo pavlenko; 55 Shutterstock/Haywiremedia; 57 Shutterstock/DGLimages; 58 Shutterstock/Blue Planet Studio; 60 Shutterstock/UmFOTO; 61 Shutterstock/Claire Plumridge; 62–63 Shutterstock/David Dennis; 65 Shutterstock/Christian Mueller; 67 Shutterstock/SteAck; 68 Shutterstock/Henri Koskinen; 69 Shutterstock/Anna Chudinovskykh; 71 Shutterstock/Zepedrocoelho; 75 Shutterstock/Katepax; 77 Shutterstock/Denis Belitsky; 78 Shutterstock/Radu Bercan; 79 Shutterstock/TonelloPhotography; 80–81 Shutterstock/ErethoroN; 83 Shutterstock/olmarmar; 84 Shutterstock/WDnet Creation; 85 Shutterstock/Boltenkoff; 87 Shutterstock/Hellen Grig; 89 Shutterstock/ziche77; 91 Shutterstock/ju-see; 93 Shutterstock/Bildagentur Zoonar GmbH; 95 Shutterstock/Brum; 97 Shutterstock/Markus Gann; 98 Shutterstock/Repina Valeriya; 99 Shutterstock/seeyou; 101 Shutterstock/mycteria; 105 Shutterstock/happyphotons; 107 Shutterstock/Phawat; 109 Shutterstock/Canon Shooter; 110 Shutterstock/Zhukova Valentyna; 112–113 Shutterstock/Tanes Ngamsom; 115 Shutterstock/framedbythomas; 117 Shutterstock/Ruslan Ivantsov; 118 Shutterstock/gorillaimages; 120 Shutterstock/Parinya Feungchan; 121 Shutterstock/Daria Arnautova; 123 Shutterstock/anthony heflin; 125 Shutterstock/fuujin; 126 Shutterstock/The Len; 129 Shutterstock/Kelly Headrick; 131 Shutterstock/solarseven; 135 Shutterstock/Aphelleon; 136–137 Shutterstock/luri; 139 Shutterstock/A3pfamily; 140 Shutterstock/Africa Studio; 142 Shutterstock/Maya Kruchankova; 143 Shutterstock/StratfordProductions; 145 Shutterstock/IMG Stock Studio; 146 Shutterstock/Gorodisskij; 147 Shutterstock/Arcady; 149 Shutterstock/eakkaluktemwanich; 150 Shutterstock/muratart; 153 Shutterstock/iravgustin; 155 Shutterstock/Mayer George; 156–157 Shutterstock/LaMiaFotografia; 158 Shutterstock/Vadven.